Nobbut a Yellerbelly!

*A salute to the
Lincolnshire dialect*

Alan Stennett

with illustrations by Richard Scollins

COUNTRYSIDE BOOKS
NEWBURY BERKSHIRE

Designed by Peter Davies, Nautilus Design
Produced through MRM Associates Ltd., Reading
Typeset by CJWT Solutions, St Helens
Printed by Information Press, Oxford

*All material for the manufacture of this book
was sourced from sustainable forests.*

CONTENTS

ACKNOWLEDGEMENTS

My thanks go to the listeners of BBC Radio Lincolnshire; Maureen Sutton; Mike Hodgson and 'Wink'; Titch Rivett; Alan Dowling; the late Rev Bill Baker; and all the others who have worked to preserve the dialect; and to the many friends and acquaintances who have offered words – sometimes of wisdom, but always of interest. Finally I must thank Sue for steadfast support.

Picture credits

The picture on page 35 is from the Local Studies Collection, Lincoln Central Library, and those on pages 25, 28, 37, 47, 51, 54 and 56 are from the Museum of Lincolnshire Life, both by courtesy of Lincolnshire County Council. The picture on page 39 is by courtesy of the Spalding Gentlemen's Society. The picture on page 9 is by courtesy of R.W.M. Dickinson. Other pictures are from the author's collection.

Steep Hill, leading down from Lincoln Cathedral

INTRODUCTION

What is Linkisheer?

A reeul eyeubbel plairce
Fer you furrinus, it's taim to larn yersen abart Linkisheer.
Doant git mardy, jus stop jifflin an oapen yer lugoils.

Lincolnshire is big, especially if you were a Roman soldier marching the 75-mile length of Ermine Street from Stamford to the Humber, or a small child crossing the Trent at Dunham and expecting to see the sea, which is still 50 miles away at Skegness.

The real Lincolnshire, *'fra' th' Wesh to th' Umber, an the Treyant to th' noth Seya'*, as one of my radio jingles used to style it, was once the second largest county in England, yielding pride of place only to the big brother to the north.

Like Yorkshire, historic Lincolnshire was divided into three ridings: *Lindsey* occupied the north and the higher and drier parts of the east; *Kesteven* took up the higher ground south of Lincoln and west of the Witham and the fens; and *Holland*, tucked away in the south-east corner, consisted of varying proportions of land and water, depending on the state of the tide and the weather.

It is, as everyone knows, flat — except for the Wolds, the Heath, the Lincoln Cliff and various other less-than-level portions. The visitor who has just struggled up the appropriately-named Steep Hill to Lincoln Cathedral appreciates the difference, as did the lady who had come to live on the edge of the Fens 'because the hills were flatter'.

Almost everybody since the Romans has passed the county by, to the complete satisfaction of many of the locals. The Great North Road and the railway main line touch the south-eastern corner and then cross the Trent into Nottinghamshire. But the folk who do pass our way have made a big impression.

Early settlers changed the virgin forest to one of the most farmed landscapes in the world. They cleared the woods for their crops and livestock, but the soil erosion that cultivation caused dumped large amounts of silt into the wetlands of the south. The local environmentalists must have hated them.

The Romans gave the county its road network, based on Ermine Street and the Fosse Way, and drivers in the county grumble that no one has improved it since.

Newport Arch in Lincoln – the only Roman gateway still used by traffic

They also established, or developed, many of the towns. Lincoln itself, *Lindum Colonia* in Roman times, was an important regional centre; Caistor, Horncastle, Sleaford and Grimsby all had settlements or fortifications; and there were smaller centres and single villas all over the county.

As the Romans left, the Danes arrived. The coronation of King Canute took place in Gainsborough while the Danish army wintered there, and a local story has it that the waves he tried to turn back were not on the coast, but the *Airguh* or *Hayguh*, the tidal bore that sweeps up the Trent from the Humber.

The Danes settled in much of the county, judging by the number of *-by* or *-thorpe* endings on our village names, the largest number to be found anywhere in the country. On their arrival, the Normans promptly fell out with Hereward the Wake, who left his home in Bourne to harass them from the relative security of the Fens. The Danish population didn't take kindly to William's arrival either, but after a couple of good thumpings in the north of the county, they stopped protesting, and Norman rule eventually prevailed. *Domesday Book* shows that Lincolnshire had one of the highest populations in England, and was a stronghold of 'sokemen', usually seen as relatively free tenant farmers.

Later incursions into the county were less belligerent, but very important. Wool traders from the continent encouraged the breeding of the Lincoln Longwool sheep, the biggest native breed in Britain, and Lincoln and Boston, the second most important port in England in the Middle Ages, held the 'staple' rights to be trading locations for wool exports.

Getting away from it all in Skegness

The Dutchmen who came to the Isle of Axholme, the Marsh and the Fens physically changed the landscape – or waterscape – of the county. Drainage and land reclamation had been going on since Roman times, but engineers and workmen from the Netherlands came in with big ideas and big money provided by local groups of 'adventurers'. Many stayed in the county, and the architecture of towns like Spalding still show the clear influence of Dutch householders who wanted to feel more at home.

The last great invasion of Lincolnshire is still going on today, as thousands of holidaymakers head for Skegness, Mablethorpe, Sutton on Sea, Cleethorpes and many other towns and villages along the coast. They came first with the railways and later by car, but they still find the breezes as *'brairsin'* as the Great Northern Railway's Jolly Fisherman suggested in the 1880s.

One other major influence on the county has been the Royal Air Force. Nearly 40 training and air defence airfields were established in the county during the First World War, although some were little more than a farmer's field left as grass with a resident airman whose job it was to clear away any livestock if an aircraft needed to land.

The new bases included the future Royal Air Force College at Cranwell, originally set up by the Royal Naval Air Service as an airship training centre, and a road at the college, Lighter Than Air Road, still commemorates that history. The

(Picture courtesy of R.W.M. Dickinson)

college was given the name HMS Daedalus, combining the interesting image of a warship marooned in the middle of the Lincolnshire Heath with the name of one of the world's less successful fliers!

Air activity reduced sharply during the years between the wars, but it was the county's role during the Second World War, as the main base for Lancaster bomber raids on Germany, that gave it the name it still carries proudly: Bomber County. By the end of that war, nearly 50 RAF stations were operational in Lincolnshire, the majority of them flying the legendary four-engined Avro Lancaster heavy bombers.

The drainers, tree fellers, farmers, sheep breeders, ploughmen, holiday entertainers, airmen and others are all still here, in what must be the most man-made county in Britain. We are a mixed lot, we yellerbellies, with shifting allegiances to East Anglia, the Midlands and the North, depending on where we are and what we do, but with a clear idea that this big lump of land, sticking out into the North Sea and once defended by bogs and rivers, is somewhere different and special. *This caps owt, mayat* – It's the very best, my friend.

Alan Stennett

CHAPTER 1

Talkin' Linkisheer

Pinning down the Lincolnshire dialect can be a problem. The size of the county, and the geographical divisions in historic times meant that different strands of the dialect developed in different areas. One expert claims that in a country area a dialect changes every 25 miles or so; this should give Lincolnshire about six, which isn't very far wrong.

Go to the south of Spalding and you're nearly in Norfolk, and you'll hear it in the speech. On the Humber coast it shifts towards Yorkshire, and Grimsby people have a whole host of specialist fishing words that would probably be well understood in Hull or even Aberdeen, but probably not in Grantham. The Isle of Axholme was almost completely cut off from the rest of the county by the Trent, and it tends to Sheffield and Doncaster for its sounds and words, and in Grantham you'll hear an East Midlands 'Ey up, mi duck' nearly as often as a Lincolnshire 'Nah then, mayat'.

Even in the heart of the county you will find that there are at least two dialects – Wolds and Marsh, and Fen – but they do have a lot in common, although there are exceptions to almost every rule. The most obvious changes are the stretching out of some vowels and the shortening of others, often the same vowel, but in different contexts.

The *a* in **bath** or **dance** is short (as in **mat** or **cat**) but in **wash** and **grass** it can become *wesh* or *gress*. At the opposite extreme, **mate** and **lake** become *may-at* and *lay-ak*. Just to confuse the issue, **make** is *mek* in some parts of the county and *may-ak* in others, and *tay-ak* and *tek* are both valid forms of **take**.

I becomes *ay* in words like **fight**, making it sound like **fate**, but it can switch to a longer *ee* sound in **night** or **right**, becoming *neet* and *reet*, or even *neeyat* and *reeyat*. Get far enough south, and you'll hit an East Anglian *oi* : *noit* or *roit*, but I don't like to confuse you too much; I am trying to be helpful. The *o* in **rope** or **slope** stretches out to *–ow* (*row-ap*, *slow-ap*); while *–ow* itself can be *–oo* or an *–aw*: **cow** is *coo*, but **crow** is a *craw*, but you don't **open** something, you *oppen* it. We don't mess with *u*; they all sound much the same: like the vowel sound in **foot**. If a Linkisheer speaker ever found it necessary to discuss the **lute**,

he wouldn't quite make it a *lut*, but it would be on its way there, and the sound an owl makes starts to approach that of a small building.

Word endings can get cut short, with *-tch* becoming *-k* (thatch as *thak*, pitch *pik*, etc) while *-dge* can be cut to *-g* (as in *rig* and furrow, the rolling farm land of alternating ridges and furrows); *-ce* is also sometimes hardened to *-ch* (so a *dunch* would have to stand in the schoolroom corner), and *-ing* is almost inevitably reduced to *-in*.

An *h* (or as a Lincolnshire dialect speaker would almost certainly say a *haitch*) at the start of a word is often lost, but the situation is confused by the fact that where standard English would use *an*, as in **an apple**, in Lincolnshire an *h* gets slipped in, so it would be a *happle*. Thus, a man from *Airceby* would be *yettin' a happle*, a phrase which also shows the alternative to an *h* in that situation, which is a *y* before an initial *e*, as in *year* (the things you listen with), and *yettin'*, which satisfies hunger. (Just occasionally, the *n* of *an* does appear, often to add emphasis to the word, but it usually gets stuck on the front of a word that would otherwise have had an *h*: *a nedge*, for instance, might surround a field, if the speaker was emphasising that it was a hedge, rather than a fence or a dry-stone wall.) *H* can also turn up, particularly in front of I (first person singular), to add emphasis: *Hi hayunt* is an emphatic refusal to do something; and *Hi hallus does* something would be in response to a suggestion that a job had been forgotten.

We may seem to have ambivalent feeling about *h*, but we do like to give it its proper place in one location that the rest of the country seems to forget. The *h* in **when, whey, whisper** and the like is pronounced, or breathed, but I can't think of a way to write that down to show the difference.

Double-d (*-dd-*) can be pronounced *th* in Lincolnshire (rather as in Welsh), turning a **ladder** into a *lather*, but it can also go the other way, so **path** is *pad*.

Past participles in Lincolnshire are often short and strong. Famously Maggie Thatcher used *frit* to suggest that her opponents in the House of Commons were scared. Many folk would say she should *nivver ev wint theer*. A Lincolnshire person who *wed* his garden hadn't married it – he had removed the weeds, and he didn't need a lawyer to *sue* some wood – he'd have done it himself with a saw. *Fust it snew, then it thew* would mean that snow had fallen, but had then melted away. The past is mutable in Lincolnshire!

Where was that?

As is probably the case everywhere in the country, place-names get modified, partly by dialect and partly by usage or laziness. Who would bother with Potter Hanworth, when you can slip *Porranuth* out so much more easily? In general, the more local, and the more rural, the more likely it is that a dialect pronunciation will be used, but 25 years of local radio in the county and a lot of *furriners* coming in have reduced the usage of some of the broader versions, especially where someone else in the county would not know where you were talking about.

BBC Radio Lincolnshire would not use Porranuth, but there was a big discussion about Louth. To Luddensians, and in dialectic, it is *Lowuth*, but the received pronunciation version is used. By contrast, the residents of the Ermine Estate in Lincoln insist that the second syllable on Ermine is pronounced as if coal was dug there, and the local pronunciation is broadcast, but the Roman Road, Ermine Street, still gets the short *-min*.

Burgh picks up two quite distinct variations only a few miles apart; it is Burruh le Marsh, but Bruff on Bain, with *Domesday* recording them as Burch and Burg respectively. Others to watch for, especially if you are a new local radio broadcaster hoping to avoid hysterical laughter in assorted parts of the county include the following:

Cowbit	*Cubbit*
Osbournby	*Ozzonby*
Folkingham	*Fockinum* (although political correctness is slipping in, and it may become another Uranus)
Aslackby	*Ayzelby*
Quadring	*Kwaydring*
Kirkby la Thorpe	*Kirby Laythorpe*
Hougham	*Huffam*
Saltfleetby	*Sollerby*

Silin' down: the Weather

Lincolnshire is farming country, and so it's not surprising that the weather is an important contributor to the local dialect. What is more surprising is that in this, one of the driest counties of Britain, words for mist and rain are much more common than any other weather terms, but more people grumble about the weather than sing its praises, so when you want a word to describe, for the tenth day running, what a rotten time you've just had in the *tayaty* field, or *gappin' beeyat*, a bit of flexibility is always useful.

The weather here is often *doley* (dull); *mawky* or *slattery* (changeable, with showers); or *mizzlin*, (a cross between a mist and a drizzle); and, as it gets progressively wetter, and muckier underfoot, it becomes *mothery, murky, drinjy* and eventually *owery* or *howery*, when the clouds close in and the *rayun* is always in your face, regardless of which way you are facing.

If the rain gets really stuck in, it progresses from *pepperin'* (a sharp shower),

NOBBUT A YELLERBELLY!

All squad and blather: the dryuh sighud o' Britain

through to a whole range of terms for heavy rain – *teamin'*, *putherin'* or *juggin'* all refer to heavy steady rain, as does the most Lincolnshire term, *silin'*, recognisable to anyone who has seen milk pouring through the filter in a sile.

If it is windy as well, then the rain will be *peltin'* into your face, and it is *skelchin'*, *culchin'*, *kelchin'* or *kelshin'* down in a heavy storm. Either way, you'd end up *wetchered* if you were caught out in it. *Rayannin' ferks tieyuns downards* does give the idea of the stinging drops hitting you in the face.

Depending on who you are, and where you are, rain doesn't have to be unwelcome. To a farmer, in spring, sunshine and showers are just what he needs – *reeyul grawin' wethuh* – especially if the showers come in the *forenoon*, but, if you've got to be out in it, it might be *catchin'* weather – liable to catch you out and give you a *sowakin'*.

Sea-mists on the coast share the terms *harr*, *sea-harr* or *hoar* with much of the rest of the East Coast, and a mist or light fog inland would probably be *moaky* or *roaky*. If it gets really heavy, it would be *thick es a puddin'*, or *clear foggy*. Clear foggy may sound a bit double Dutch, but 'clear' here means completely, and also turns up in *clear dull* 'totally overcast' and in *clear black* for a starless night.

14

Cowd or *caud* are fairly obvious, and *raw* can be used if it is damp as well, but there is also the specifically Lincolnshire term *clam* for cold and damp. A sharp frost would be a *ray*, and could result in roads that were *slayap wi' ice* and hedges covered with *riyam*.

If it really *clems up*, like it did in 1947 or 1963, you may well be out thawing pipes, carting water out to livestock or clearing roads with a tractor. In the 1947 freeze, the railways in the county were badly affected; so some bright spark had the idea of mounting a couple of the newly invented (in Lincolnshire) jet engines on railway wagons to clear the snow. They did blast their way through the drifts, but, unfortunately, they also blew away most of the track ballast and a fair amount of signalling equipment as well.

The bitter, biting east wind that carves its *snide* way across the Fens in winter would have come *strairt fra Siberia*. Anyone working out on the land in January or February wouldn't need to be *nesh* – a bit soft about being cold – to be *starved* or *nithered*. If the wind is blowing *snaw* with it, the snow *windles* its way into *reeyaks* or drifts. Before the snow actually starts to fall, that heavy, pearly-grey sky could be *gleeanny*.

Keeping the draughts out could be a full-time occupation in a farm house or a worker's cottage, and a cold wind blowing through an open door might get a

Jet engines on railway wagon in snow

blunt *'Put wud in th'owul!'*, or it could provoke the question *'D' ya cum from Baardney?* ', based on the story that the monks at Bardney Abbey always left their doors open, after refusing to open them one night for the bones of St Oswald.

Draughts might be a particular problem if the wind was *brisslin' on a back-endish day* 'blowing gustily about on a damp and chilly day that reminds you that the muds and cold of autumn will be along before too long'. While a very hot day might be a *razzler*, or *gleeyammy* – so bright that everything shines like new, with lots of reflections off surfaces – but if it gets *clowus* 'hot and sweaty', it could be *smudgy, mulfrey, munskey* or *clunch*.

'Weather', used on its own, always means bad weather in Lincolnshire. *Wethuh is cumin'* means rain, snow, wind or cold, never a bright sunny day!

It probably sounds as though we yellerbellies are inveterate grumblers about our weather, which may be true, but it could also be that we keep the best of our conditions to ourselves. Our big skies are our great glory, whether they be studded with clusters of high clouds in a brilliant summer blue or resplendent with Orion and the winter stars on a frosty December night. To a true Lincolnshire person, there isn't much that can compare with a brilliant dawn coming up over the East Coast, when the light reflects off all the streams and inlets and the marshland *bodds* start to get about their business, or a magnificent *bullfinch sky*, a glorious deep red sunset, marking the end of the day.

The Lincolnshire Show always takes place close to the summer solstice, and there is something special about watching the sun go down late in the evening of the first day as you enjoy a drink and a Lincoln Red steak over a barbecue in the stockmen's camp, and then being woken with the dawn the next day as those same stockmen get out to *tittivayat* their animals before the championship judging. *It's a reeyull treeyat, mayat.*

17

A Local Skem at Nursery Rhymes

The Grand Old Duke of York

CHAPTER 3

Linkisheer Dictionary

Compiling a Lincolnshire dictionary is a difficult task. Very few words are exclusive to Lincolnshire, and some of those that are, are only known in parts of the county. Lots that are fondly thought of as dialect are old family words, known to nobody but a particular family, but vigorously defended against any charge that they are not genuine Lincolnshire. (Words for bodily functions often turn out to be family inventions, which may account for some of the vast number of euphemisms in circulation.)

The following is a selection drawn from personal recollection, suggestions by others and from a variety of other sources, some of which are rather ancient and may include words no longer in use. However, they should give a feel for the language, but for a wider choice, try Joan Sims-Kimbrey's *Wodds and Doggerybaw*.

If you happen to be reading this in Norfolk, Yorkshire or the East Midlands, and recognize a word, please look after it, use it carefully and send it home in good condition after you have finished with it.

ablins	perhaps
addle	to earn
	Addle yer bread.
afoor	before
ageeyan	against or next to; not opposed to
Ah /ah	I, but also he or one; a sort of all-embracing pronoun
allust / hallus	always
ann'all	as well
'an't	have not
argify	of importance
	It doan't argify. 'It doesn't matter.'
awming	wasting time; idling about

axe	to ask
	She axed fer a penny.
ayabul	well set up for money
	My Great Uncle Abel was a jeweller and watchmaker and had to put up with references to how *Abel* was *ayabul*.
ayam	frost that forms on the inside of a window
ayl stang	See **stang**
'ayp'uth	literally, a halfpenny worth; virtually nothing
	'E 'an't a 'ay'puth o' sense.
ayun't	is not
back end	autumn or winter
bang	exactly
	bang in the middle
battle-twig	an earwig
bawks	big timbers, wooden beams
bedstock	a bedstead
bees	flies
	The bees is as fell as owt. 'The flies are very bad.'
beeyaverin' away	beavering away: working hard
beneyan	below
bested	beaten
beyastins / beyastlins	
	colostrum: the very rich milk from a cow that has just calved
	Can be made into beastins pudding or custard (an acquired taste)
blatherment	nonsense
	Poettery is a screeyad of blatherment an' waarse.
blobbin'	fishing for eels with pieces of cord or fabric as bait
blowed	surprised
	Ah'll be blowed!
boggard	a ghost or bogeyman
bogglin' abowut	messing about

bor / boy	like mate, a greeting
	Nah, bor!
born days	life
	all me born days
bowak	to be sick
	'Ead owermuch beyar an' bowaked i' th' streyat.
brig	a bridge
brock	dried cattle dung used for burning. Also **casson, cowsan**
brog	to jab or make holes with a stick
bully	a sloe, fruit of the blackthorn
butterbump	the bittern
cap all / cap owt	to be better than anything
casson	See **brock**
cat-lap	1. any weak and watery drink 2. nonsense
	Doan't gimme thet cat-lap.
causey	paved path or yard
cetchin' gawp-seed	
	standing with the mouth open in amazement
	Ef ya stan' theeya cetchin' gawp-seed, foalks'll think ya're soft i' the 'ead.
chop	to swap or exchange
clap gate	a kissing gate
clemmed	held; gripped
clink and clean	completed well
clivver clogs	clever clogs, know-all
clot head	idiot, probably originally cloth head
clout	a cloth
clunch	morose, uncommunicative
cotted	tangled
cowsan	See **brock**
cramble	to walk slowly and/or stiffly
create	to make a fuss
	Dowant creeyate so.

cross 'oppled	confused
cute	intelligent, sharp
dacker down!	Slow down; don't get over-excited!
darklins	twilight
dilly / dilly-cart	a cart used to remove the contents of a privy
dinkum	a share of work; *fair dinkum* a reasonable division of work (according to a north Lincolnshire source quoted by the Australians)
doggerybaw	nonsense
door darn	door post
dussun't	doesn't
ennew	enough
far-weltered	1. turned on its back (of a sheep); 2. in north Lincolnshire, tired out or beat
fat tiger	boiled fat bacon with very little lean in it, served cold
fen nightingale	a frog
fitties	an old term for a marsh, used in Lincolnshire for a group of chalets and bungalows built on reclaimed land near Cleethorpes
flit	to move house
flittin' day	See **pag**
forr'ard	forward
fra	from
frit	frightened
frummerty	frumenty: a pudding made by boiling wheat in milk
fun	found
gansey	a jumper (possibly a corruption of *Guernsey* denoting the thick oiled wool jumpers worn by fishermen)
gel	female equivalent of **bor**
gizzen after	to look out for someone you fancy *She was gizzenin after th' mester's lad.*
glegg	to look at
gommeril	idiot
gooly	the yellow hammer

hobby horse	a dragonfly
hot aches	the burning sensation when very cold hands start to warm up
howats	See **wotts**
huck	the hip (part of the anatomy)
hutch up	to move along, either to make space or to get closer to someone
ivins	ivy
jifflin'	fidgeting
kek	the white-flowered wild plant also known as cow parsley or Queen Anne's lace
kelch	a blow
	'E cot me a kelch roun th' lugoil.
kelter	rubbish, mess, useless things; a wife's view of her husband's collections
	Wot's yon lowad on owd kelter?
kest	south Lincolnshire equivalent of **far-weltered** (1)
lantron	a lantern
larrup	to beat
	a good larruping
leaf	the fat lining a pig's intestines
lether	a ladder
letten	left; allowed
	'E 's letten 'em goa.
lig (on)	to lie on

Lincolnshire bonnet

a type of women's headgear designed to avoid sunstroke or an unfashionable tan while working outside

(Courtesy Museum of Lincolnshire Life)

lodnum / lodlum	laudanum, an opium derivative used to counter the ague or malaria
maddock	a maggot. Also *mawk*.
	Scrayap th' mawks of th' bayacun afore they yet in.
mangalayated	mixed up
	Farmworker explaining how a grain drier works: *Hayer (air) blaws in heyar (here), grayun gowas in theyar, an it all gits mangalayated.*
mardy	grumpy, irritable
mashlin bread	bread made with a mixture of grains—wheat, barley, oats could all be used, depending on what you had to hand; poor man's fare
mawk	See **maddock**
mawkin	scarecrow
	'E loooked a reglar mawkin.
mayablins	maybe, possibly
moastlings	usually
mowdywarp	a mole (the animal)
mun	must
neb	a beak; a person's nose
nivver not	not under any circumstances
	Double, or even treble negatives in Linkisheer just emphasize the situation: allus *nivver reet; I ain't nivver not goowin' to doo it.*
nobbut	only, nothing but
	There be nobbut two sooarts o' chaps - them as likes doin' ard werk an them as likes to see 'em do it.
nowat	nothing
nunty	Grimbarian for old-fashioned, boring, or just 'not cool'
oarts	leftovers
odling	something unique
okkers	heavy boots
oppen	open

ort	(in speech) nought, zero
	'Is phowan number is ort wun fower.
otchin	hedgehog (perhaps from itching, because of the load of fleas a hedgehog carries)
owd	old, also as a term of affection; our *owd boy* or *our owd gal* could be son or daughter, a wife or any other close relative
pad	a footpath
pag	to carry, usually on your back
	Pag Rag Day or **flittin' day** (14th May or thereabouts) was when farm workers moved to a new job, carrying all their clothes and other belongings with them.
parson	a signpost
peeyaz	peas or pears (take your pick!) Work it out from the context, though, as the 'Two Ronnies' showed, a tin o' peeyas could be either. (It might also mean the opposite to war, but that would be closer to *peeyass*.)
petty	a privy or lavatory—the outdoor kind with one, two or three holes
pig	the woodlouse
pink	the chaffinch, also **pollypink**
pissabed / pissbed	the dandelion (an effective diuretic)
pissmire	an ant (from the smell of an ant-hill)
pode	a frog or toad
poke	a bag
	A young pig could be carried to market in a poke.
pollypink	See **pink**
potato	a hole, as in a sock or a sleeve
pudge hoowal	a rut or depression that quickly fills with water when it rains and slowly drains away afterwards

Kechen' podes
(Courtesy Museum of Lincolnshire Life)

puttin' away	dealing with the meat after a pig killing
pyewipe	plover, lapwing
raave up	to drag out past arguments or differences
rammel	hard core; rubble; broken bricks, stones
ramper	a main road, often on a causeway across low-lying land prone to flooding
rantan	See **stang**
reeyak	a snow drift
reeyasty	fat that has started to go off
ribbon tree	the birch (from the way the bark peels away)
rightle	to correct, put right
rigtree	the beam that supports the ridge of a roof
rowadd	apart from the obvious, also a direction: *Goa that rowadd*, or personal space: *Git outta rowadd an' let me git on.*

salary	celery
sarmint	a sermon
	Yon Methody sarmints gooer on ferevver.
sayame	pork lard or dripping
scran	meagre or poor food
scraps	the small crisp pieces left when meat has been rendered down for dripping; the pieces of fried batter from a fish shop
sen	self, as in *missen, yoursen, hissen*
sewer	sure, certain
skem / sken	to look closely
skiyuv	to look innocent
skrawk	to write
	Old-fashioned dipping pens were known as *skrawkers* when I was at school.
sliyuth / sliyuv	to sneak about
smoot	a passage
sneck	a latch, door fastener
snicket	an alleyway; short cut
snook out	found (having looked for)
spadger	the sparrow
spit	a spade depth
splauts	feet
skwad	mud
stang	a pole
	An *ayl stang* was a pole with a metal fork on the end for catching eels, but *riding the stang* was a way of showing community disapproval of a wife-beater: someone representing the culprit was carried past his house on a pole while neighbours *rantanned* – beat pots and kettles with sticks.
stitherum	confusion
	all of a stitherum

stunt	awkward, stubborn, difficult
	Dooant be stunt.
suzzy	a pastry turnover, e.g. a jam suzzy
swinehaw	the blackberry
taaitie	a potato. Also *tayate*
taaitie- / tayaty-trap	
	the mouth
taffle	a tangle
tayacken	spoken for or chosen; engaged (to be married). When two captains choose a team for football, those already picked would be described as *tayacken* (taken).
tayate	See **taaitie**
telled	told
thack	thatch
tharms	pigs' intestines used for sausages
thrif / thruf	through
thunderwort	sempervivum, the house leek
	When growing on a roof was supposed to protect against lightning.
tongue-banger	a nagging person
tood	tired, out of breath, exhausted
	A cow that had just had a long calving would be *tood*.
turn	(of fruit) to ripen
underneyan	underneath
uneppen / unheppen	
	clumsy
varmint	vermin
vittals	victuals, food
wad / wowad	woad
	Until 1932 woad was grown in the fens as a dyestuff, not just for Ancient Britons to 'fit on'. The smell of the fermentation process was so noxious that Elizabeth I forbade its production within five miles of any of her houses.

washboard	not something played by Lonnie Donegan, but a term for skirting board, designed to protect the base of walls from damage and from damp when swilling or mopping the floor.
weeyant	will not
	Ah weeyant goa ta skoowul.
while	until
	Legend has it that locals waited at barrier level crossings until the lights flashed, and then tried to cross. It is also reported to have caused problems for the children at a non-Lincolnshire school when their new Lincolnshire teacher told them that they wouldn't learn anything while they listened to her. Since she might also have told them she would *larn* them, rather than teach them, the confusion would have been complete.
wikkin	a corner
	th' wikkins o' 'is mowouth
wok	work
wolds	high, uncultivated land (Old English *wald* `forested upland'; compare German *Wald* `forest')
wud	mad
	'Eed gone cleyan wud. 'He had gone totally mad.'
yak / yowak	oak
yeart / yet	to eat

On the farm

artificial	manufactured fertiliser
	Th' fowerty hayker wants a dressing o' artificial.
ask	hard and dry, referring to the ground. Also **hask**
	Yons too ask ter pluff it naow.
bat / batten	a bundle of straw
beealin'	the noise cattle or a calf makes when hungry; a baby's crying
beeyasts	beasts, usually cattle; animals

bottle o' hay	a bundle of hay tied up for carrying
boy's land	light land, easy to work
breead	the width of one pass of a scythe or similar agricultural implement
breeyad 'n' cheeyas	hawthorn leaves when young and tasty
cad yard	a knacker's yard, where dead livestock are disposed of
carf	a saw cut in wood
cart	a two-wheeled vehicle (Compare **moffy, wagon**)
cart hovvil	an open-fronted shed in which carts and wagons were kept
cayad	an abandoned or orphaned lamb or other baby animal
chick / chit	a sprout on a potato or seed
clowas	field (plural: *clossen*)
corf	a calf
cow paddle	an area for grazing cattle

Wagon dressed for 1919 Victory Parade

The site of the first Lincolnshire Show was the Cow Paddle in Lincoln.

crew	an enclosed, strawed, cattle yard
drayap	drape: a cow with no milk
fleeyak	a wattle hurdle
footing	payment to a new worker
fother	fodder: horse food
gablick	a crowbar that is square in section with a point on one end, used for fencing

A hole was made with the point, and then the post was knocked in using the gablick two-handed.

gaffin' up	feeding and bedding livestock in the evening; settling them down for the night
gang mester	gang master: the supervisor of a group of workers
garth / gath	a cattle yard
garthman	a stockman
godfeyther	an angled support placed against a post at the end of a wire run or at a corner in order to counter the pull of the wire
graayan	grain
graayav	a heap of potatoes or other root crops, covered with straw and earth to protect it from winter conditions. Also *pie*
gress	grass
grip	a shallow trench dug to allow water to drain from a road or a field
hale	a plough handle
hask	See **ask**
havvers / hayavers	wild oats
jacker / jackstraw	a straw elevator
jiggul-pin	a rod that held a tip cart in place

When you pulled the pin out, the cart tipped.

leyadin'	leading: carting, bringing in

To lead muck or beet, for example, was to cart it to or from the fields.

mashlin / maslin	mixed grain
moffy	a two-wheeled cart which could be converted into a four-wheeled wagon

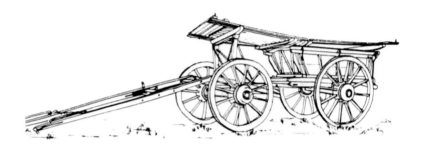

outliggin'	the practice of leaving cattle out over the winter
pie	See graayav
pine	to starve
pingle	a small area of land
pining shed	an area near a slaughterhouse in which animals were kept without food before being slaughtered
plash	to lay a hedge
	This was done by cutting out the thinner branches, and then cutting part way through the stems to that they could be interwoven to create a stock-proof barrier.
podder / poddert	a sheep older than a lamb, but not full grown; a hogget
reckling	the smallest pig in a litter
rig	ridge
scarry	to break up ploughed land using a set of harrows
scotch	a block placed under a wheel of a wagon to stop it running away
scuttle	a wide shallow tub or basket used in a stable or for carrying grain
sex	bags for grain, (singular: *seck*)
shottle	a moveable rail in a fence
skelp	to tip a cart in order to empty it
slaayap	slippery

slyav	to sneak in
	'E slived in thruff th' back dooer.
spud bashin'	potato picking
	Originally, this involved pulling the plant and knocking the roots together to get the soil off.
stayul	stale: (of a horse) to urinate; horse urine
stoowuk / stowk	stook: 1. a set of grain sheaves stood together to dry in the field. 2. to arrange sheaves in a stook
	Stowk 'em up teet, else wind'll blaw em dowun agin.
straddle	the flat base of a stack
tent	tend: look after animals
traya	a wooden hurdle
tunnup	turnip
unicorn	a trio of plough horses, one in front of a pair
vollunteeyar	volunteer: a crop seed growing as a weed in a later crop
waarpin'	the practice of letting silty floodwater flow over land to improve its fertility
wagon	a farm vehicle with four wheels (Compare cart)
wagoner	the head horseman on a farm
wheeyat	wheat
wotts	oats. Also **howats**
wozzle	a mangold or swede
yerk	a leather strap or twine tied round the trouser leg just below the knee in order to stop the trouser bottoms dragging in the mud (or to prevent a rat running up your leg).

(Courtesy of Local Studies Collection, Lincoln Central Library)

yoe	ewe: a female sheep
yon	that
	Yon yoes far-weltered.
yok on	to attach a trailer or implement

Countin' sheeyap

In every area where sheep were kept, shepherds had a system for counting them that didn't use conventional numbering. Lincolnshire was no exception, but the exact terms varied within the county and beyond. The following is Farmer Wink's version.

1. yan	11. yanadik
2. tan	12. tanadik
3. tethera	13. tetheradik
4. fethera	14. fetheradik
5. pethera	15. bumfit
6. lethera	16. yanabumfit
7. severa	17. tanabumfit
8. overa	18. tetherabumfit
9. covera	19. fetherabumfit
10. dik	20. diggot

Some sources say it then goes on to *yanadiggot,* and so on, but Wink says: 'Nah! Yah just notch yer stick an' staart agin.' Other people picked up a stone with each 20, put it in their pocket and then counted up in *scoowers.*

Children deciding on the order of something would use *foggy* for first; *seggy* for second, or *thirdy* for third.

Down the fen

banker	a workman digging or clearing drains
batter	the slope of a bank

Yer say yer lef a yoe 'ere this mornin'?
(Courtesy Museum of Lincolnshire Life)

bear's dung / bear's muck

a mixture of clay and decayed reed exposed when cultivating or ditching

beck   a stream

brush out   to clean dead twigs and rubbish out of a dyke

carr   (in the north of the county) land drained for cultivation; sometimes specifically land liable to be flooded by salt water

clough / clow / cluff

a set of gates in a drain that allow water to flow out, but not back in again

creek / crick   an old stream bed filled with silt

croomin' pole   a combined hook and rake for clearing weeds out of a waterway

dales   on the Witham fens, reclaimed land allocated to a village: Martin Dales, Timberland Dales.

decoy   a duck trap

delph   a drain, with banks, emptying into another drain; on the Witham Fens particularly, a straight cut to take upland water across an area prone to flooding

dike reeve / dyke reeve

an official responsible for checking the condition of drainage and flood control works

drain   a drainage channel larger than a dyke. Also *lode / layad*

Clough on Metheringham Delph

dyke   a small drainage channel

ee   a drain; sometimes spelt *eau*, but the French pronunciation is not historically correct. Also *eya*

engine   a pump

engine drain   a drain leading to a pump

eya   See ee

faggot   a bundle of sticks or brush used to reinforce drain banks or flood defences

fen   land drained for cultivation (from Old English *fen(n)* 'marsh')

fleet   an inlet or shallow stretch of water, usually tidal

gote / gowt   the point at which a drain or canal empties into a river. Also *tydd gote / gowt*

Anton's Gowt links the River Witham and the navigable drains near Boston.

graff   a drain, often marking a parish boundary

hodding spade   a wide, shallow-bladed spade for work in wet conditions

ing / ings   boggy grassland

layad / lode	See **drain**
pullover	easier slope on either side of a bank to allow wagons to be drawn over it
punt gun	a large bore, long-barrelled gun that was mounted on a punt and used to fire a big charge of shot into a flock of waterfowl on the water or rising from it

(Courtesy of Spalding Gentlemen's Society)

rodden	a ridge in the fen where peat has shrunk away from both sides of a stream bed, leaving it raised above the ground
sewer	an old word for a drain
	The Woodhall Sewer passes the site of the ancient fishponds of Kirkstead Abbey and would have been the Kirkstead sewer.
slodger	a worker in the fens, sometimes using stilts to travel in flooded areas
squad / skwad	thick sticky mud
tydd gote / gowt	See **gote**
wath	a ford
watter jawled	flooded

Sum Linkinsheer sayins and expressions

a lick and a promise
a quick wash

all of a stitherum   in a state, worried, confused or upset

all over the okshun

> all over the place, usually as a result of a mishap
>
> *'E trippt an' it went awl over the okshun.*

all squad an' blather

> 'all mud and confusion', i.e. a general mess

allus lookin' aware

as daft as a boiled owl

> completely useless

as mad as a Stamford bull

> very angry
>
> Bull-fighting went on at Stamford until the 18th century.

as neyar as mayaks nowt

> pretty close

ayn't backards in cummin' forr'ards

> a bit pushy

back o' beyon' hard to get to, though not necessarily a long way away.

> Sots Hole, down Metheringham Delph, could be *at th' back o' beyon* even though it is only about five miles from Lincoln.

bad to th' bowan irredeemable

bullfinch sky a red sunset (from the colour of the bird)

bury wi' 'am to give a good funeral with a proper tea

cum ovver all unnecessary

> to feel embarrassed

fair ter middlin' satisfactory

get shut on to get rid of

get the thick end of someone's tongue

> to be told off

He could git under a snayaks belly wi a top 'at on.

> Don't trust him!

He's gone to Botany Bay.

> I don't know where he is, or when he will be back.

Hive got a craw ter pluck wi' you.

I want to discuss something with you, or express my disapproval.

I'll go to our 'ouse!

I am surprised.

I've been eggin' back o' Doids.

Grimsby term for `mind your own business'; an answer to the question Where have you been?

The story has it that people used to collect seabirds' eggs from the shore behind a business called Doids.

Nah then!   the standard greeting

on the slosh   at an angle; poorly placed

A badly parked vehicle would be on the slosh.

a pump weeyout a nandle

a useless or incompetent person

pleeased as a dog wi' two tails

very happy

Them as 'as 'as; them as 'assunt 'assunt.

a recognition of economic reality

Thur en't noah pockits in a shrowud.

Money's no good to the dead.

upset yer apple-cart

disrupt your plans

What in tarnation?

What on earth?

when bodds 'as two tayals

spring, when birds with forked tails like the swift and swallow reappear

Yer've got nagnails in yer knickers.

You are fidgeting, fretting or twitchy.

CHAPTER 4

Dialect Humour

Two Lincolnshire lads are lost in the desert, dry as a bone and starved. 'Lawdy, Joe, wot we gointa do?' asks one. 'If a doan't git summat t'yet soon a'll dwine awaay.'

They crawl to the top of the next dune, and he looks over and says, 'Look down yonder. Thuzz a hoasis wi a baacon tree.'

'Doant ya talk cat-lap, Bert,' says Joe. 'Thuzz noah sich thing as a baacon tree.'

'There is—thuzz wun down there, and arm gooin' to git me a feed.'

So off he went, and came back all scratched and scarred and bruised, and Joe says 'Nah then, Bert, was it a baacon tree?'

'Noah, you was rait. It wern't a baacon tree, it was a hambush.'

The vicar was walking past Fred's garden, and stopped to admire the splendid display of flowers.

'That's a wonderful show you've got there, Fred,' he said.

'Ay, its tekken me a fair bit o' wok,' Fred replied.

'You've had some help from God, though.'

'Aye, but 'e's not much ev a gairdner, as you'd ev knowed if you'd sen it when 'e 'ad it all to issen.'

A Wolds farmer had just bought a new bull, and the farmworkers from all around were coming to have a look at it.

The garthman got a bit fed up with all the comin' and goin', and told the man in the yard to charge the visitors.

'Mek em all paay a penny—summ'ull be sceered off, 'n' us'ull mek a bob or two outen the huthers.'

'Ah cairn't affud a penny, mester,' one would-be visitor complained, 'Ah've got twelve kids at hooame.'

'Chaarge the huthers a penny, but let thiss'un in freyah,' the garthman said. 'But mek shoeer the bull gits a good look at 'im. He miyut larn it summat.'

The farmworker was looking a bit green about the gills, so his mate asked what was wrong.

'Well,' he said, 'Ah was doasing th'oss wi' a pill and a tuwubb to blaw it down its throwat, but th'oss blowed fost.'

Owd Bill Smith was being harassed once again by the lady from the council who wanted him to stop using the old outdoor petty and have an indoor WC installed. Bill was not convinced that he wanted to have that nasty, unhealthy object inside and was refusing to cooperate.

'But Mister Smith,' she finally burst out. 'It hasn't even got a lock!'

'It dooan't need no lock,' Bill replied. 'It's nivver had no lock for fowerty years, and nobbody's stooalen a bucketful yit.'

CHAPTER 5

Yettin' Chine

Traditional Lincolnshire food is basic stuff. It is mostly 'country food'; straightforward belly-filling grub, based on what could be produced from a pig and a plot, to keep a farmworker supplied with energy through a day singling beet in a bitter east wind *cummin strayat fra' Siybirria*, as my uncle would have put it. In its simplest terms, it could be boiled down to 'We eat the whole pig, and most other things that come along as well'.

Grain was, and still is, one of the main farm products of the county, so bread would always have been a staple of the diet, but it would not always have been a modern white loaf. Stoneground wholemeal made from a variety of grains all went into bread, and although the modern dietician would approve, the abrasive nature of some of it made a major contribution to the gap-toothed grins of many a local. Wheat and rye were both used for bread, but oats and barley also featured, with some references to pea flour down on the fens. In early days, the loaves would have been prepared by the housewife, and then taken to a village bakehouse to be cooked, but the bakehouses evolved into bakeries, offering bread for sale, and better cooking facilities in the home would include an oven to allow home-baking.

Sweetened breads are still popular in the county, with Lincolnshire plum bread – usually served with cheese – a key part of any traditional county event.

Plum bread, or plum loaf, could be any kind of dough sweetened with dried fruit, ranging from a near-normal loaf with mixed dried fruit, similar to the Welsh *bara brith* (literally 'speckled bread'), to a rich concoction that would not shame the name of a full-scale fruit cake.

My mother's recipe falls towards the richer end of the spectrum, although she would never consider it the equal of her fruit cake!

Lincolnshire Plum Bread
1/2 lb butter
3/4 lb sugar
1 lb dried fruit
1 lb self-raising flour
1/2 teaspoon bicarbonate of soda
1 cup cold water
2 beaten eggs

Melt the butter in a pan, add the sugar and fruit, and mix well. Cool the mixture with the water and add the eggs, flour and bicarb.

Pour the mixture into two 1lb loaf tins (give the bowl to the children to clean out – unbaked cake mixture was a childhood treat) and bake for ½ hour at oven Mk 3; then reduce to Mk 2 for a further 1½ hours until browned on top and of a consistency to appeal to the family.

To keep with tradition, serve buttered, with cheese, but it is very acceptable as an unbuttered cake.

Another local sweet 'cake' is Grantham gingerbread, although ginger biscuit might be a better term. The local story is that a baker in the town was preparing a batch of Grantham whetstones, a hard biscuit designed to sustain travellers by coach on the Great North Road, but incorporated ginger by mistake. The rest is history, as are Grantham whetstones.

Flour, along with eggs, fat and milk, also went into puddings, but the modern image of the sweet treat at the end of the meal is not appropriate. Puddings were fillers, served at the start of the meal, to reduce the appetite for the more expensive meat of the main course. The idea that they can't have any meat until they finish their pudding would puzzle my grandchildren, but it would have been quite normal to my parent's generation.

Steamed puddings or something like a suet jam roly-poly would have been regular offering, as would batter puddings. My grandmother used to make something she called pancake pudding, which was a kind of Yorkshire pudding

with dried fruit. The recipe has been lost, but would be gratefully received by me if anyone still makes it.

* * * * *

A vital use of barley before the arrival of clean water was the manufacture of beer and small beer, the main drinks of the whole household.

One of the guides at the Epworth home of the Wesley family, the founders of Methodism, enjoys pointing out that John and the others were regular beer drinkers.

'Why do you think that was?' he asks visitors, who usually offer the technical answer that the fermentation of the beer kills off bacteria in the water, thus leaving a less contaminated drink.

'Well, that may be true,' the guide responds, 'but the real reason is that they weren't Methodists yet, so nobody said they couldn't.'

Most families would have had a garden or a vegetable plot to provide potatoes, root vegetables, cabbage, Brussels sprout, cauliflower, peas, beans and virtually everything else that appeared as a vegetable on the dinner plate.

Fruit from a garden or an orchard would be eaten in season, converted into jam, or preserved, along with any surplus vegetables that would not store. Pickling and bottling were key skills for the housewife before the invention of the deep freeze.

Tayates, or *taaities*, would have been part of most main meals, usually boiled or roast with the meat. My dad would eat some fried left-over potatoes, providing my mum didn't try to incorporate too many vegetables, but he looked with suspicion on jacket potatoes, and chips were something you bought from a chippie. The key role of the potato as a food and as a commodity, is shown by the old couplet:

When at last the fenman dies, and comes to Heaven's gate
He'll ask the angel at the door 'Now, what's the price of tates'?

Meat for the main meal might be beef or mutton, which would usually come from a local butcher, although there are stories of farm workers in the wool-producing parts of the county complaining about the amount of old mutton they had to eat. The meat of an old ram, killed because he was too old to carry a full fleece, is not an attractive proposition, and the Lincolnshire Longwool was always bred for wool rather than meat.

Some families kept geese, but the true friend of the cottager or the village dweller was the pig. Almost everybody kept a pig, bought as a suckler early in the year and fattened on plenty of boiled taaities, household scraps and anything else that came to mouth through the year before its inevitable demise in the winter. The traditional Lincolnshire Curly-Coat pig was a massive animal, which could weigh up to 4 cwt (200 kilos) at eight or nine months old. It had been developed as a bacon pig from what Mrs Beeton's *Book of Household Management* refers to as 'the Old Lincolnshire breed – long-legged, weak in the loins, with coarse white curly hair, and flabby flesh', but its descendants were bacon machines par excellence.

The pig could almost be a household pet, and many a country child has had its first hard lesson on the reality of life when the pig he or she has fed with the odd treat, chatted to and scratched the back of through the year met its end with much frantic squealing and struggling. As recently as the 1980s, a neighbour of mine kept a pig in a sty in his back garden, to which I fed large numbers of surplus apples, bowls of potato peelings and other things, just for the pleasure of seeing it pop up on the sty wall and grunt what my anthropomorphic leanings heard as a greeting. I felt very bad when it was killed, but I didn't turn down the *pig-cheer* when it arrived a day or two later.

Pig killing, or *puttin it awaya*, was a time of great ritual and tradition. My father was a butcher before the war, and took up the trade alongside his farming when he came out of the army in the 1940s. It was a still a time of rationing; so the formality of the occasion was enhanced by the presence of the local

Pig killing
(Courtesy Museum of Lincolnshire Life)

policeman, there to make sure than an extra pig wasn't slipped through the system and put on the black market.

The pig would have been *pined,* or starved for a day before killing, and then brought into the slaughterhouse, in my dad's case, or to a suitable location for the killing and initial treatment. It was held on the *cratch* – a cross between a trolley and a sack-barrow – and killed by slitting its throat with a very sharp knife, inserted into *the stickin playerce* at one side and drawn straight across the jugular vein. It was important to get as much blood out of the carcase as possible, and the shoulders could be pumped to help the flow. Lincolnshire was not great black pudding territory; so the blood was usually washed away. Hair and scurf were removed by soaking in hot, but not boiling, water and scraping the skin: too little water, or too cool, and the hair stayed in place; too hot and you started to cook the meat. An alternative to scraping was to drag a chain along the carcase several times, which was reported to do a good job.

The head was then removed and put on one side, and the carcase washed down with cold water. To be able to work on it, the pig was hoisted up by means of a *cammeril* – a piece of wood shaped rather like a bucket yoke – between its back legs, and hung from a beam or a tripod. One or two cuts the length of the belly allowed the *innards* to be removed and sorted for future use. The intestines would be rinsed in salted water and cleaned as *tharms* and *chitterlings* for sausage making; the stomach went for tripe, although it needed a lot of rinsing and soaking to get rid of a rather bitter taste; the lungs, or *pluck,* went into the mince; fat was put on one side for rendering into lard; and the brains, heart, liver, kidneys and sweetbreads all went into the *pigs fry.*

Pigs fry was a neighbourhood tradition. The bits from the innards were mixed with about the same amount of pork trimmings from the carcase to make plates of *pig cheer,* which were distributed to your neighbours, in the expectation that you would get the same in return when they killed their pig. The empty plate had to be returned unwashed to the originator.

Pigs fry

My own recipe for pigs fry is to dust the meat with seasoned flour and fry it with some onions. When it is browned, add water to cover, and cook until tender. Serve with potatoes and a green vegetable. Easy stuff and very tasty. My wife prefers to roast the floured meat pieces for a while to crisp them, before simmering in water, but without the onions; the end result is much the same.

Mayakin bayacon

The bulk of the meat was then preserved as bacon joints. My father had big lead-lined troughs (I later made off with the lead and sold it to a scrap dealer for 6d/lb, big money in the 1950s!), in which a couple of inches of dry salt was laid. The meat was put rind down on the salt, with a little saltpetre rubbed into any bloody joints. More salt was poured on top of the joints, and rubbed in. It was left for a day or two, and then turned and more salt added and rubbed in. After a few weeks, the joints would be taken out of the troughs and hung up to dry, sometimes in muslin bags or even old cotton pillow cases. Hung in a dry room (look for the hooks in the ceiling of an old farmhouse kitchen), they would keep well, although it was sometimes necessary to scrape off a bit of mould or cut away an infestation of maggots.

The *chine*, along the back, was reserved for *stuffed chine*, a special occasion treat. The chine was soaked to get rid of some of the salt, and then scored deeply with a sharp knife down to the bone. The trick was to get the cuts as close together as possible without the joint falling apart. The cuts were then stuffed with chopped parsley — about a bucketful to a decent chine — wrapped and tied in an *owd cotton bed sheet* and boiled for several hours. Other leaves were sometimes included, but a traditional chine just used parsley. It was served cold, with vinegar, pickles or pickled samphire, a plant found along the marshy parts of the coast. Stuffed chine was the special meal, traditionally served at May Day, christenings and other notable occasions, when it was a matter of pride to get the appearance right as well as the taste. As one friend explained to me, 'Me Dad sez its just like mekkin' luv to a bootiful wooman. However much you've 'ad, you can allus manage a bit mooore. 'E cudd yet stuff chine fower tiyums a day, an still ax fer moore.'

Most bacon was eaten as boiled bacon, hot at dinner time and cold for breakfast, tea and supper. It could be anything from a fairly lean, meaty cut to a thick slab of almost pure fat. We knew the fattest cuts as *fat tiger*. Others had less appealing names for it.

The reeyal treeyats

What was left of the pig went into a variety of dishes. The best fat — *leaf* or *kell* fat — was rendered down for dripping or lard, to be stored in the pig's bladder, with the bits of fat eaten as *scraps* with a shaking of salt. Any other fat that wasn't needed for specific dishes was also rendered down.

Other meats went into sausages, haslet, pork pies, and brawn. A proper Lincolnshire sausage is seasoned with sage, and an attempt is being made to have it recognized as something special to the county which should be made here only. Haslet — *acelet, airslet*, or however else you like to pronounce it — is similar, but includes darker meat, liver, sage and other seasonings, all wrapped in

the *apron*, the tissue mesh that holds the internal organs in place, and baked.

Pork pies, to me, mean Christmas. Pig killing was usually a pre-Christmas job, both to save having to buy food to keep the pig alive in the winter and to ensure an adequate supply of *vittles* for the festive season. Baked in a hot-water pastry crust, with set jelly between the meat and the pastry, pork pie with toast is my Christmas breakfast.

I did check with my mother about a recipe for pork pies, and I offer it as guidance rather than a rule.

Pork pies

'There will be about a stone of meat, with salt and pepper, so you make enough pastry to cover them – about 7lb plain flour, 3½ lbs lard, 1¾ pints boiling water and some salt. If you need more pastry, just increase in proportion. Make up your pies in tins and send them to the village bakery, since you'll have too many for an oven. They taste better that way anyway.'

The meat for the pie needs to be cut up rather than minced, which the 19th-century dialect writer Mabel Peacock claimed would be '*a squeezin' all goodness oot 'n meyat*'.

Brawn

The final dish is probably the least seen now, and the contents may explain its rarity. *Brawn, jelly, collared head or collared rine* was a kind of jelly incorporating the rest of the head, the ears, the trotters and any bits of rind that had been cut away. They were boiled until the meat fell off any bones present. The bones were removed; the rest was chopped and boiled again, then allowed to set. It was served at breakfast or tea.

Food for free

What was produced in the pen and the plot would be supplemented by the produce of the countryside. Blackberries, nuts and mushrooms could be picked, as could the seashore plant samphire. As well as being pickled to eat with stuffed chine, it could be eaten fresh, boiled and served with salt and melted butter, with the fleshy parts of the stems drawn off between the teeth and butter running down your chin.

Many wines and fruit syrups could be made from fruits and flowers, and young nettles, dandelions and other wild plants appeared regularly as vegetables or in soup.

Fish could be plentiful, as could game, but hunting or catching it was fraught with risk. Landowners wanted to keep it for themselves, and employed

Gathering samphire
(Courtesy Museum of Lincolnshire Life)

gamekeepers to make sure they did, but pigeons and rooks, considered pests by the farmers, were indeed 'fair game', and catching rabbits, as they broke free from the last patches of uncut corn, delivered both sport and nourishment to the men and boys working in the fields.

In a good year, the Yellerbelly ate well; in a bad one, he wouldn't usually starve, but he could get pretty hungry and more than a bit bored with his food.

CHAPTER 6

Linkisheer Specials

'**T**he Lincolnshire Poacher', the county song and parade march of the Lincolnshire Regiment, also gave rise to the second-favourite nickname for Lincolnshire folk: *poachers*.

When I was bound apprentice in famous Lincolnshire
'Twas well I served my master for nigh on seven years
Till I took up to poaching as you shall quickly hear
Oh, 'tis my delight on a shiny night in the season of the year.

As me and my companions was setting out a snare
'Twas then we spied the gamekeeper, for him we didn't care
For we can wrestle and fight, my boys, and jump from anywhere
Oh, 'tis my delight on a shiny night in the season of the year.

As me and my companions were setting four or five
And taking them all up again, we caught a hare alive
We caught a hare alive, my boys, and through the woods did steer
Oh, 'tis my delight on a shiny night in the season of the year.

We threw him over my shoulder, boys, and then we trudged home
We took him to a neighbour's house and sold him for a crown
We sold him for a crown, my boys, but I divve't tell you where
Oh, 'tis my delight on a shiny night in the season of the year.

Success to every gentleman that lives in Lincolnshire
(Alternatively: Bad luck to every magistrate)
Success to every poacher that wants to sell a hare
Bad luck to every gamekeeper that will not sell his deer
Oh, 'tis my delight on a shiny night in the season of the year.

Lincolnshire Livestock

Lincolnshire may well have been the only county to have its own complete set of farm animals: Lincoln Red cattle, Lincoln Longwool sheep, Lincolnshire Curly-Coat pig, Lincolnshire Black horse and Lincolnshire Buff chicken.

Lincoln Red cattle are the descendants of the Viking-type shorthorn cattle which probably came into the county from Northumberland. Local farmers selected them for the cherry-red colouration and developed 'a breed of cattle ... unsurpassed in this country for points highly valuable and for their disposition at any age to finish rapidly', according to the Board of Agriculture in 1799. It was formally established as a breed in its own right just over a hundred years ago. The Lincoln has suffered from the competition of faster-growing continental breeds, but its marbled, succulent meat is now making a comeback as a quality product.

Lincoln Red

Lincoln Longwool sheep are Britain's biggest native breed, with the longest staple, or fibre, of any breed. It was the foundation of the county's wealth in the Middle Ages. Wool, 'the Sovereign merchandise and jewel of this realm of England', was shipped through the 'staple towns' of Lincoln and Boston to markets all over Europe, and many of the fine churches of the Lincolnshire Fens and Wolds owe their quality to the generosity of wool farmers and merchants, one of whom had engraved on his window 'I praise God, and ever shall, it is the sheep have paid for all'.

When Robert Bakewell set out to create his New Leicester sheep breed, he took Lincolnshire Longwools and crossed them with his local Leicestershire animals. Ironically, when the Lincoln breeders later wanted to improve their breed, they took the Leicesters and introduced them into their stocks. This genetic merry-go-round improved both breeds.

The Lincolnshire Curly-Coat pig is, sadly, no longer with us. The last animal died some time in the late 1960s or early 1970s, just before the cavalry of the Rare

Curly-coat Pig
(Courtesy Museum of Lincolnshire Life)

Breeds Survival Trust rode in to save threatened breeds of British farm animals. It was the last to be lost.

It was a pig bred to fit the needs of a working farm population; it was massive, very fat, able to live on virtually anything that could be spared from the farm, garden or kitchen, and able to supply most of the meat needs of a family for a year. A cut from the belly of a Curly-Coat would probably turn a modern consumer as pale as the block of almost lean-free meat itself, but that fat would keep a farm worker supplied with energy over a long, hard, cold day in the field. Legend has it that there are still Curly-Coats to be found on farms in Hungary, where they were taken to improve the local curly-coated breed, but several expeditions from Lincolnshire have failed to find them!

The black horse of the Fens – the Lincolnshire Black – is also no longer with us in person, but its descendants can be seen wherever heavy horses are still at work. The breed was one of the foundations of the Shire horse, still a favourite of enthusiasts for the gentle giants.

The Lincolnshire Buff chicken also died out in the 20th century, but since its origins were known, a group of enthusiasts have recreated the breed, which has been featured in a leading poultry magazine as the 'chicken that came back from the dead'!

Mud and stud

Lincolnshire has a number of mud and stud buildings, constructed of timber frames – the studs – covered and infilled with mud – a mixture of earth, lime, straw, cow dung and horse hair. The name is unique to Lincolnshire, but similar techniques have been used elsewhere, including at the historic Jamestown settlement in the United States.

It is often confused with wattle and daub, but the system does have significant differences. Wattle and daub uses a woven mesh of willow onto which the daub is spread, while mud and stud used a series of vertical wooden 'studs', with the mud packed between them to make what is virtually an earth wall, with very little support from the wood. The whole was usually topped off with a thatched roof, extending over the walls to reduce the chances of damage from heavy rain. The walls are usually whitewashed, again to give protection against the weather.

Genuine mud and stud buildings are quite rare, but Lincolnshire has many houses that were mud and stud and that were modernized in more recent years by the replacement of the mud with brick panels. Though a more weatherproof

A mud and stud cottage
(Courtesy Museum of Lincolnshire Life)

material, brick offers few of the thermal benefits of mud and stud, which stayed relatively cool in summer and held the internal heat in winter.

A fine example of the technique is Withern Cottage, at the Museum of Lincolnshire Life's Church Farm centre in Skegness. The building was removed from its original location in the nearby village of Withern and reconstructed at the museum. I was one of the people privileged to join the process of adding the mud to the structure during a radio outside broadcast. To ensure adequate sound effects on the radio, it was essential to slap the mixture on with some vigour, which we did. We chose not to ask the precise components of the mix, but it was a very entertaining session!

Stamford: the town that should have had a county

Stamford is a beautiful, stone-built town tucked into an odd little pocket on the far south-west corner of Lincolnshire. It is an important town: a communications centre before the coming of the railways; a major market for the area; and even a rival to Oxford and Cambridge as a university location, but by all rights it should have been best known as the county town of

Stamfordshire. The other four of the five towns of the Danelaw – Lincoln, Derby, Leicester and Nottingham – became county towns, but Stamford gives the impression that no one knew quite what to do with it; so it was tacked on to Lincolnshire.

Logically, Stamfordshire should have included that other surprising oddity, Rutland, by far the smallest county in England, along with Kesteven and possibly those less-inundated parts of Holland west and south of the Witham, with the rest added to Lindsey. According to one theory, it lost out because Rutland was the personal territory of a Mercian queen and was therefore left intact when the county structures were first drawn out. Another theory is that the defences of the long Lincolnshire coast required the resources of a bigger county to maintain them. Either is possible, but we are unlikely ever to know the answer.

Woodhall Spa

Some 200 years ago, the pretty Victorian town of Woodhall Spa did not exist. The man who is often credited with creating it, John Parkinson, was a man of high ambition, even for Lincolnshire. He is said to have had three ideas: to build a city, plant a forest, and dig a coal mine. He established his 'city' at New Bolingbroke in the newly drained West Fen, which still boasts an attractive crescent of houses at its centre. The forest was established on Kirkby Moor, and he set out to dig his mine in what was to become Woodhall Spa.

Sadly, his ambitions outran his pocket, and he went bankrupt. New Bolingbroke and the woods were sold, and the mine failed to find coal and was abandoned in 1824 when the workings flooded. A few years later, when the waters flowing from the shaft were analysed, they were found to be rich in minerals, and the spa was established. It thrived for nearly a century, during which several large hotels were built, and the town was planned 'on an approved English system, and suitable to refined English habits'.

The spa declined after the First World War, and, although golf took its place as a local attraction, it avoided much of the architectural change of the 1950s and 60s. It still offers the visitor a pleasant stay, with the opportunity to pay a visit to the Kinema in the Woods, virtually unchanged since it was established in 1922 by the conversion of a sports pavilion. It may be the last working back-projection cinema in the country.

The triangular bridge at Crowland

In the middle of the small town of Crowland, close to the ruins of the magnificent abbey, is a 13th/14th-century bridge where three roads meet over three arches, through which flows nothing at all.

Old Bridge, Crowland, Lincolnshire.

It appears that it was once a functional bridge at a point where two streams merged into one, but drainage of the area and the diversion of the waterways mean that no water now flows under the pointed arches, and the roadways are too narrow for anything bigger than a horse.

At one time there was a cross on the bridge and a place for pilgrims to stop and pray.

The Hood

Take a Fool, a Lord, who is also a Chief Boggard or Boggin, eleven subsidiary Boggards or Boggins, a hood and the cheerful denizens of several pubs in Haxey and Westwoodside in the Isle of Axholme, and you have the Hood, or the Haxey Hood.

Held on 6th January, Twelfth Night, or old Christmas Day, the Hood is a village game claimed to date back to the 13th century, when Lady Mowbray lost her hood in a high wind. It was caught by a group of farmworkers, and returned to her. It must have been a valuable garment, because Lady Mowbray is supposed to have given land and money for an event which has been celebrated ever since.

There are links between the Hood and the Plough Jags, plays and performances to commemorate the turn of the year; the Fool and the Lord tour the pubs in the area beforehand as part of the Jag celebrations, inviting participants to join in the Hood. On the day itself, all the 'officials' dress up, the Fool in a large flowered hat, clothes decorated with red patches and what looks rather like red and black warpaint, and the Boggards in red coats, or at least wearing some kind of red symbols.

A drink or two is taken in one or more pubs before they depart to the churchyard, where the Fool stands on a particular stone and makes a speech welcoming visitors and inviting them to join in. The speech includes the invocation '*Toon agin toon, hoose agin hoose, If thou meet a man, knock 'im doon, but dooan't 'urt im*'. During the speech, a fire of damp straw is lit under the Fool to '*smoke*' him, a safer version of the traditional approach, in which the Fool was tied to a branch of a tree, swung back and forth over the fire, and then dropped in. Legend has it that on one occasion in the 50s someone forgot to dampen the straw and the Fool caught fire, but he was apparently extinguished with no great harm done.

Everybody then leaves for the traditional field, and a few practice hoods are thrown just to get everyone in the mood. Eventually, the main hood, a two-foot long leather-wrapped sausage, is thrown into the centre of the crowd, and the *sway* begins. The idea is to get the hood into your particular pub, and when that happens there are great celebrations and a lot more beer, often provided free by the winning landlord, who then keeps the hood on display till the following year.

The hood cannot be thrown or kicked, it must be *swayed* – pushed or dragged – and having up to four 'teams' taking part does complicate the direction that you might choose to push towards. A cunning team can use another to push in their general direction before trying to make a break for their own 'goal', but the others are usually aware of that possibility and action will be taken to block it.

Nothing is allowed to impede the progress of the hood, which has been known to destroy hedges and demolish stone walls, but one of the Boggards' jobs is to make sure no one is trapped under what is effectively a very large scrum, and they can pause the action to avoid injuries. The whole process usually takes a minimum of two hours, but has been known to go on well into the evening.

Given the time of year the Hood takes place, the field is usually pretty muddy and may still have a crop residue in it. The last time I went down, the crop had been Brussels sprouts, and the thick stems were still standing. The sound of a breaking sprout stem is very similar to that of a breaking limb, adding an extra dimension to the general havoc.

CHAPTER 7

Linkisheer Place-names

Scratch the surface of any town or village in Lincolnshire, and it's likely that the Danes, or their fellow north Europeans, have had a hand in the founding, naming or development of it. A Danish farmer buying land there in the county in the 21st century said that he felt quite at home, since 'Jutland shares history with Lincolnshire'. It was only a thousand years ago ...

The county saw many waves of immigrants during the six centuries following Roman rule, although there is still much debate as to whether they came as mercenaries hired by local rulers who then took over, as raiders arriving by sea to take what they could, or as settlers moving into relatively uninhabited areas. The answer is probably all three, at different times and in different circumstances. The Saxons were here as Roman mercenaries as the empire declined, and their influence grew, more or less peacefully, as friends and families joined them. More belligerent groups from Scandinavia, mainly Danish, arrived later, and the extent to which they dominated the county is clear from their influence on village names.

The overall history of settlement in Lincolnshire can still be traced by its place-names, with newcomers establishing villages, or changing the names of the ones that were there already. We don't seem to have a Lincolnshire equivalent of Torpenhow in Cumbria, which means 'hill hill hill' in three successive languages, but we do have other linguistic mixes, including the county town itself.

THE ROMANS

Lincoln is a fairly straightforward derivation from the Roman name *Lindum colonia*. A *colonia* was a settlement for retired soldiers – a kind of Cheltenham-by-Fen – but *Lindum* itself is probably a derivation of a pre-Roman name possibly meaning '(place) by the pool' (compare Welsh *llyn* 'lake'). The place-names Caistor, Ancaster and Casterton all show Roman influence, Old English *caester* denoting a Roman fort or encampment, although both Ancaster and Casterton carry later additions that indicate they were close to a Roman camp rather than a continuation of it; so Casterton would be a homestead (Old English *tūn*) by the old camp, and Ancaster could indicate that the owner of the land around it was a man called Ana or Ane.

THE 'DANES'

The biggest influence on Lincolnshire place-names came from the Norse or Old English of the residents in the centuries after the Romans left or were pushed out, depending on your view of history, and the languages of the assorted Scandinavians who followed them into the county, usually lumped together as 'The Danes'.

Lincolnshire has more place-names ending in -*by* (from Old Norse *by*), indicating a farmstead or a village centred round that farm) than any other county in England, with at least 205 villages or hamlets carrying it, from Aby to Wrawby. These include:

Aby	farmstead or village by a stream or river; or eel farm
Barrowby	on a hill
Boothby	with shelters (hence possibly a seasonal or temporary settlement)
Boothby Graffoe	= Boothby + an old district name
Boothby Pagnell	= Boothby + the manorial prefix from the Paynel family
Carlby	the free peasant's farmstead
Coningsby	of the king
Grimsby	of a man called Grímr
	The local story is that Grim(r) was a fisherman who rescued the son of the king of Denmark from a boat. He named the child Hablock, or Havelock, and brought him up. When the child grew up, he was returned to his parents, who rewarded Grim(r) with enough goods and money to return to Lincolnshire and establish the town which is named after him. The town's seal includes the names of Grim and Hablock.
Kirkby	farmstead or village by the church
Normanby	of the Northmen or Norwegians
Skendleby	by a beautiful slope
Thorganby	farmstead or village of a man called Thorgrímr

Ulceby (several examples)

	of a man called Ulfr
Welby	by a spring or stream
Wickenby	of the Vikings or of a man called Vikingr
Willoughby	by the willows

borough 'fortified place', 'stronghold' (Old English *burh*, dative *byrig*)

Alkborough	stronghold of a man called Alca; or possibly on a ridge or Alka's farm
Gainsborough	of a man called Gegan

bourne 'stream' (Old English *burna*)

Aubourn	eel stream
Redbourne	reedy stream
Welbourne	stream flowing from a spring

fleet 'inlet of the sea', 'estuary'; 'stream' (Old English *flēot*)

Saltfleetby	farmstead or village by the salt creek, or the creek from which water was drawn for salt production
	Preparing salt from seawater was an important industry in Lincolnshire from before the Roman times up to the Middle Ages.
Wainfleet	Probably linked to a wagon as in the hay wain, but just possibly a survival of part of the old Roman name of Vainona

ham 'homestead, farm or village' (Old English *hām*)

Grantham	gravelly or sandy village
Threekingham	most likely the village occupied by Thirkle's people
	Local legend, however, claims it as 'three kings village'. According to the story, a great battle was fought in the 9th century against the Danes at nearby Stow Green. Victorian sources name the victors as Algar, chief of the Mercians, Wilbert, and Leofric, although they add that yet another use

of the old trick of a fake retreat by the Danes led to their defeat shortly afterwards. The bodies of the defeated Danish leaders are supposed to be buried in mounds alongside the main road, close to the church, while Algar is commemorated, and possibly buried, at Algarkirk.

holm / ey 'island', 'raised land in a marsh' (from Old Norse *holmr*; Old Norse *ey* or Old English *ēg*)

Axholme	is a large area in the north of the county which is virtually surrounded by the rivers Trent, Idle, Humber, Yorkshire Ouse and Don. Its name may come from the village of Haxey, or share the same meaning: 'island of a man called Hákr'.
Bardney	island, raised land of a man called Bearda
Blankney	island, raised land of a man called Blanca
Gedney	pike island
Sibsey	island, raised land of a man called Sigebald
Torksey	island, raised land of a man called Turog

-ing-   'the people or followers of'

Billingborough (*Billingeburg* in *Domesday Book*)

    fortified place of Bill(a)'s followers; alternatively, stronghold on a ridge (Old English *bil(l)ing*) the village is on the first stretch of rising land to the west of the Fens.

Billinghay (*Belingei* in Domesday Book)

    island, raised land of Bill(a)'s followers

Hagworthingham (*Hogberdeingham* in *Domesday Book*)

    village of Hogberd's followers

ness 'promontory', 'point' (from Old Norse *nes* or Old English *næss, ness*)

Skegness	headland of a man called Skeggi
	Longshore drift has moved the headland further south to Gibraltar Point, now an important national nature reserve.

thorpe 'secondary settlement' or 'outlying farm' (Old Norse *thorp*)

Kettlethorpe   outlying farm, settlement of a man called Ketil

toft 'homestead' (Old Norse *toft, topt*)

Bratoft   broad homestead

Brothertoft   sounds too simple to be true; more likely to be from a name rather than a sibling

Wigtoft   homestead by a creek

ton 'settlement, farmstead, village' (Old English *tūn*)

Boston   farmstead or settlement of Bōtwulf

The famous Boston Stump church is dedicated to St Botolph, but the name is a later construction, since Boston itself did not come into existence before the 12th century.

Fenton   farmstead or settlement in fenland

Horsington   belonging to a man called Horsa

Owston   east (Old Norse *austr*) farmstead

Sapperton   farmstead or settlement of the soapmakers

wick / wich 'bay or inlet; port; trading, industrial, or processing centre' (Old English *wīc*)

East and West Butterwick are on the Trent, close to its outfall into the Humber.

Scopwick   sheep (Old English *scēap* 'sheep') farm

When is a gate not a gate?

A gate (Old Norse *gata*) is a road or street. The village of Crossgate lies at a road junction just north of Pinchbeck, Halton Holegate refers to the rock gap through which the road from Spilsby heads for the coast. Fleet Hargate, Chapelgate, Gedney Broadgate and Garnsgate all lie within a mile or two of each other between Holbeach and Long Sutton.

Anyone making the false assumption that the terms refers to an entrance in the town or city walls (Old English *geat*) would need to think again in Lincoln: the city has a Westgate and an Eastgate, as well as a Broadgate, Langworthgate, Exchequergate, Greetwellgate, Clasketgate, Aldergate, Michaelgate, Danesgate, Saltergate and Hungate, which would have resulted in more gates than wall.

Wormgate, Boston, with the Stump

Likewise, Spalding has Churchgate, Pennygate, Halmer Gate and Stockwell Gate; Sleaford has gates for all points of the compass, as well as a Water Gate; you can walk Eastgate, Westgate, Northgate, Chequergate, Gospelgate, Ramsgate and Upgate in Louth; Gainsborough's waterfront wharves were served by Caskgate; Grantham has a Westgate and Watergate; and Stamford apparently kept its Caledonian residents separate from the rest of the community in Scotgate. In most cases the origin of the name is clear in terms of the direction of the street, the trading that was carried on there, or the important buildings to be found there. Boston – which also boasts a Wide Bargate and a Strait Bargate – and Grimsby can perhaps claim the best gates: the splendid Wormgate, running alongside the river in Boston, and Walmsgate in Grimsby, which both translate as 'Dragon Street'!

The Danelaw

Under the Danelaw, which was established in the late 9th century, Lincolnshire became an important centre, the towns of Lincoln and Stamford being two of the five boroughs of that administration. Danish rule eventually fell to that of the English in the early 10th century but, although historians report that much fighting took place, the change was probably of little significance to anyone but a few administrators and the upper classes. The average fenman would hardly have noticed it at all, being already well established in the continuing belief that the less he has to do with the ruling classes the better.

THE NORMANS

Norman French names came into the county with the conquest of 1066 and all that, but tend to be associated with the hierarchy.

Belvoir (Vale and Castle) 'beautiful view'

Norton Disney is a nice mix of the Old English place-name meaning 'north

settlement' with *de Isney* 'from Isney', the name of a family who came over with William, and from whom Walt claimed descent.

Mavis Enderby could be Mauvais Enderby, though why it should be worse than Wood or Bag Enderby isn't clear. It is more likely to derive from the Norman French Malebiss family who owned the area in the 13th century. (It did provide excellent amusement when some kind soul saw the sign 'To Old Bolinbroke and Mavis Enderby' and added 'the gift of a son'.)

Ashby de la Launde and Grange de Lings may have similar French connections, but the paired villages of Gayton le Marsh and Gayton le Wolds and Holton le Clay and Holton le Moor appear to have very little French influence apart from the preposition. A quick translation from Gayton in the Marsh and Gayton on the Wolds may have offered a quick boost in local prestige, but not a lot else.

KEEPIN' OWUT THE WATTER

The draining of the Fens and reclamation of land from the sea has left a number of places deprived of the reasons for their names. Moulton Seas End and Surfleet Seas End were once alongside tidal water, but are now several miles from it. Holbeach Bank, Haven Bank, Lade Bank and many roads going by the name of Roman Bank attest to barriers built to stop water spreading onto the land, and many a Fenside no longer looks out over water and willows, but their name reminds occupants of what could happen if global warming takes hold.

OTHER ODDITIES

Spital in the Street is not nearly as unpleasant as it sounds. Once upon a time it was the site of a hospital, a resting place for travellers and the poor as well as somewhere for the sick, and is located close to the old Roman road Ermine Street.

Twenty is a cluster of buildings alongside the location of the long-closed railway station of the same name on the Midland and Great Northern line from the midlands to the Norfolk coast. It is said to be so bleak and uninviting a place that an additional panel was added to the Twenty sign on the main road. It read 'Twinned with the Moon: No Atmosphere'.

Tongue End is close to Twenty, and is named after the tongue-shaped spit of land between the Bourne Eau and the River Glen.

There are several farms and a hamlet by the name of Cold Harbour. They were places where travellers or tramps could find shelter, but with no home comforts like beds or fires.

Lincolnshire Overseas

Lincolnshire gave many names to the colonies in New England, including that of its major city, Boston, despite the fact that the Pilgrim Fathers were jailed in Boston, Lincolnshire. Many of their number originated in North Lincolnshire, and it is claimed that the escape was planned in the Old Hall at Gainsborough. Lincolns also abound in the USA, but they tend to be linked with the president of that name, rather than the county. The author was startled to be told by a resident of Lincoln, Nebraska that it was very good of the people of Lincolnshire to name their city after Honest Abe.

The county also brought back some names from the colonies, especially to the land which was being drained and reclaimed in the 16th and 17th centuries. There is a new New York and a Bunkers Hill close together on Wildmoor Fen, which was not drained and enclosed until the 1800s.

SOME LINCOLNSHIRE NAMES

From a list of farmers in Lincolnshire with names not found anywhere else in 1890, the following names are still to be found in the current county phone directories:

Anyan, Bett, Blades, Blankley, Border, Borman, Brackenbury, Bristow, Broughton, Brownlow, Brumby, Burkill, Burkitt, Butters, Cade, Cammack, Capes, Casswell, Chatterton, Codd, Collishaw, Coney, Cooling, Cottingham, Coupland, Cranidge, Cropley, Cutforth, Cuthbert, Dannatt, Daubney, Desforges, Dook, Dows, Dowse, Drakes, Drewery, Drewry, Dring, Drury, Dudding, Elvidge, Epton, Evison, Forman, Frisby, Frow, Gaunt, Gilliat, Goodyear, Goose, Grummitt, Hay, Herring, Hewson, Hides, Hildred, Hoyes, Hoyles, Hutton, Ingall, Ingle, Laming, Lamming, Leggett, Leggott, Lill, Lilley, Lynn, Mackinder, Maidens, Marfleet, Markham, Mastin, Maw, Mawer, Merrikin, Minta, Mowbray, Odling, Overton, Palethorpe, Patchett, Pick, Pickwell, Pocklington, Ranby, Reeson, Rhoades, Riggall, Rippon, Sardeson, Sargisson, Scarborough, Scholey, Scoley, Srimshaw, Searson, Sergeant, Sharpley, Sneath, Stamp, Storr, Stowe, Strawson, Stuble, Temple, Thurlby, Trafford, Ullyatt, Vinter, Waddingham, Wadsley, Wass, Westerby, Westoby, Whitsed, Willey, Willows, Winn, Wroot.

Only Bermrose, Elmitt, Gilliart, Gillyat and Scrimshire are no longer to be found, although they may not be listed, or not own telephones! Many of the names are still involved with farming, although recent changes in the structure of agriculture have seen many families leave the land.

CHAPTER 8

Yellerbellies

I'm a Yellerbelly. I spent the first twelve years and the past twenty-five of my life in Lincolnshire, and claim the universal nickname of Lincolnshire people. But where does it come from? It probably depends on how kind you want to be, and whether you are one or not.

It is possible that the term refers to the yellow waistcoats and uniform frogs (fasteners) worn by the Lincolnshire Regiment, or to the undersides of coaches that were painted yellow and that used to travel to Lincoln. Another suggestion is that market women kept a separate purse for gold coins tucked into their skirt waists, or had a special pouch for them in their aprons, so that a good trading day would result in a golden, or yellow, belly, but why that should be peculiar to Lincolnshire is not clear. The same applies to the idea that farm workers in the fields acquired a brown back, but that constant bending to their work meant that the belly was less tanned, and looked yellow by comparison.

Sheep might have got a yellow belly while grazing in flowering fields of mustard, but since that would result in a sharp drop in yield of mustard seed, they would probably have been chased out again long before they had a chance to change colour! That staple of Lincolnshire farm food, the cured ham or bacon hanging for too long from the rafters in the kitchen might turn *reyasty*, and it has been suggested that someone who was offered a slice took offence and applied the term to his hosts!

Many ideas relate to the Fens, and a name given to the fen dwellers could have become attached to Lincolnshire folk in general. Most people still think the county is all flat fens; so it would be an idea that might readily spread. Fen dwellers, like yellow-bellied eels, frogs or newts, were seen as spending their time in mud and water, and so it may be a 'fenmen, eels, frogs, newts – all the same thing' idea. Of these options, newts – particularly the great crested newt, now rare, but once common in the Fens – get a lot of support.

People living in the Fens were also keen growers and users of opium, to help them to fight off the malaria which was endemic in the area. The medication can turn the skin yellow if used to excess. The final, and, to some people, the most convincing suggestion, however, is that the term came from Lincoln

Diocese's Elloe Rural Deanery, covering the Fens, which took its name from the Saxon administrative division (wapentake) known as Ye Elloe Bellie.

The Fen Slodger

The true Fenman – 'Web-footed an' yellerbellied' – may seem to have had a hard life, assuming, as the great Victorian Samuel Smiles did, that they were 'an amphibious race largely employed in catching eels'. Usually wet, often cold, afflicted by malaria, addicted to opium, and living in an environment, inhabited, according to St Guthlac of Crowland, by devils of many kinds, he (or she) would hardly be a cheerful soul, would he?

Well, the truth was rather different. The Fens were not all a boggy morass. Open stretches of water and drier islands broke up the landscape, and the rich variety of the environment offered plenty of ways of sustaining life and feeding a family.

Fish and eels were available in enormous amounts. In *The Medieval Fenland*, Danby recounts that eels often served in lieu of currency, with some debts and rents paid in 'sticks', each of 25 eels. One fishery paid 14,500 eels a year in rent, and the abbey at Peterborough received 4,000 a year in return for the right to

FEN SLODGERS.

take building stone from Barnack, near Stamford. Edible birds were present in profusion, and decoys were built over appropriate stretches of water to catch hundreds of ducks and other waterfowl at a time. Records also refer to swans, herons, geese, cranes, bitterns, water crows (whatever the latter may have been) and many other fowl eaten or trapped and sold to others.

Reeds and rushes for thatching and turf and peat for burning could also be cut and sold, while, close to the coast, salt production was a valuable business. Arable land was scarcer, but, where cultivation was possible, grain, pulses and flax were grown, as well as fruit trees. Oats were important as a supplement to the diet of the large numbers of livestock that were grazed on the marshes.

It would have been a life as good as – and in many ways better than – that of most of their dry-land contemporaries, and so when the gentlemen adventurers came to drain the Isle of Axholme and the East, West and Wildmore fens, it is not surprising that many of the inhabitants objected vociferously and physically at the destruction of their way of life.

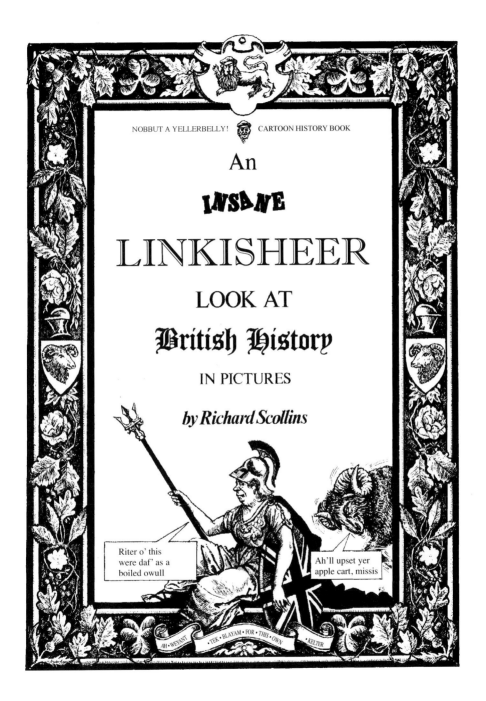

NOBBUT A YELLERBELLY!   CARTOON HISTORY BOOK

An

INSANE

LINKISHEER

LOOK AT

British History

IN PICTURES

by Richard Scollins

Riter o' this
were daf' as a
boiled owull

Ah'll upset yer
apple cart, missis

AH •WEYANT • TEK • BLAYAM • FOR • THIS • OWN • KELTER

Alfred and the Cakes – AD 878

Canute Demonstrates His Inability to Turn the Tide – AD 1020

Lady Godiva – AD 1057

The Battle of Hastings – AD 1066

The Death of William Rufus – 1100

King John and Magna Carta - 1215

Edward I Presents His Son as Prince of Wales – 1284

Bruce and the Spider – 1306

The Battle of Agincourt - 1415

Richard III at Bosworth - 1485

Henry VIII and Anne Boleyn – 1529

Raleigh and the Puddle – 1581

Francis Drake Goes Bowling – 1588

The First Night of 'Hamlet' - 1601

The Gunpowder Plot - 1605

The Execution of Charles I – 1649

Charles II and Friends Hide From the Roundheads – 1651

Isaac Newton Discovers Gravity - 1666

Bonnie Prince Charlie Arrives
in Scotland – 1745

Nelson at Trafalgar - 1805

Wellington Inspects His Troops – 1815

The Charge of the Light Brigade – 1854

Stanley Greets Dr Livingstone – 1871

Queen Victoria 'Not Amused' - 1878

BIBLIOGRAPHY

Airfields of Lincolnshire, The, Blake, Hodgson & Taylor, Midland Counties Books (1984)

Egging Back o' Doids, The Doughty Centre Local History Group, University of Hull (1995)

Fenland Landscape Glossary for Lincolnshire, A, Hilary Healey, Lincolnshire Books (1997)

Highways and Byways in Lincolnshire, W F Rawnsley, Macmillan & Co (1926)

Illustrated Lincolnshire, G J Wilkinson (pub 1900 by the author)

Jabez Good's Lincolnshire Glossary, Skegness Publicity Services (1973 reprint)

Lincolnshire, E Mansel Sympson, Cambridge University Press (1914)

Lincolnshire Country Food, Eileen Elder, Scunthorpe Borough Museum (1985)

Lincolnshire Dialects, G Edward Campion, Richard Kay (1976)

Lincolnshire Life magazine

Lincolnshire People, John R Ketteringham, Kings England Press (1995)

Records of Woodhall Spa, J Conway Walter, W K Morton, Horncastle (1908)

Medieval Fenland, The, H C Darby, Cambridge University Press (1940, and reprinted David & Charles 1974)

Wodds and Doggerybaw, J M Sims-Kimbrey, Richard Kay (1995)

The Internet: an invaluable source of information, misinformation and distraction.